M000310140

BE MY LOBSTER

& never let me go

SARAH FORD

BE MY LOBSTER

& never let me go

SARAH FORD

ILLUSTRATED BY
ANITA MANGAN

spruce

To find your lobster, you must be prepared to climb aboard the love boat, sail uncharted waters and weather the storm in search of real love that will last for now and always.

Your lobster is your one true love for life: the one that will stick around whatever, the one you will want to have baby lobsters with, the one you will bare your soul to and the one you will want to grow old with.

When you've found your lobster, you will know – and you will give yourself a little pinch, just to check that the deep joy you feel is really real. With your lobster on board, you can set sail for love island, on a trip that will last a lifetime.

8 WAYS YOU WILL KNOW YOU HAVE FOUND YOUR LOBSTER AND NOT JUST FISHED OUT ANOTHER CRAB:

1. You looked in all the right places and there was your lobster, just getting on with life in the deep blue...one touch of a claw and you were smitten.

2. Suddenly, your past is rightly consigned to history – it's all about the here and now. Bottoms up to a sunny and salty future with your lobster!

3. You find yourself looking up at clouds and seagulls rather than under rocks or in the muddy depths – the world feels much bigger and full of hope when your lobster is around.

4. You feel literally unstoppable: Team Lobster against the world!

5. You are never bored, even when you're doing nothing. Just hanging out with your lobster is the best thing ever.

6. You can be yourself and you know that is good enough. In fact, it's more than good enough...all you need is each other.

7. Your lobster is your best friend. You can share everything, safe in the knowledge that your lobster has your back and will be true to you.

8. Any bad habits your lobster may have – blowing their nose loudly or constantly running late – are overlooked as mere quirks, just part of the many facets of their utterly adorable personality.

Lobster wondered
if he could see her
heart beating.

Lobster was so happy,
she couldn't eat her pizza.

When he went away,
Lobster sent her
a message in a bottle.

Lobster had beaten
all the competition
to win her heart.

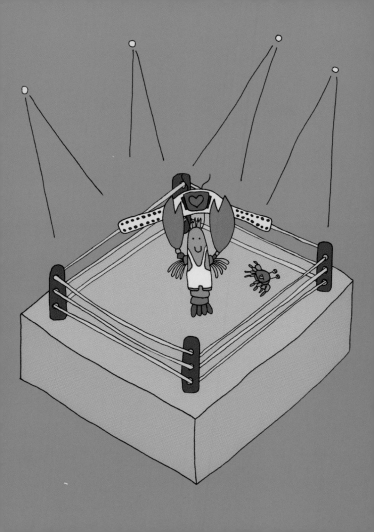

Lobster wondered how
he was going to get all this
in her packed lunch box.

All Lobster wanted to do was cup her face.

Lobster thought she
was beautiful even
with a mouth full
of marshmallows.

Lobster and Lobster
had found the
rainbow connection.

Lobster was trying
very hard not to look
at her roots.

Lobster had spent all
day making a mixtape.

Lobster was feeling
a little blue.

Lobster had made
her a shell necklace.

Lobster thought this was worth getting wet for.

Life is your lobster,
thought Lobster.

Lobster had her always
on his mind.

Lobster loved his girl
to the moon and back.

Lobster was trying
to see all of his mess
as love tokens.

Sharing spaghetti is the
best, thought Lobster.

Lobster was scratching
her back for the fifth time
in a week.

Lobster stuck an
extra cherry on top.

To mark the occasion,
Lobster shared a poem.

Lobster made her
a special glitter card.

Lobster thought it would
be boring if they liked
all the same things.

Lobster was whispering
sweet nothings.

Lobster and Lobster
sailed away for a year
and a day.

Lobster was trying
to light her fire.

Lobster had made her
his special curry.

To keep the peace,
Lobster ate the
coffee cream.

Lobster thought that
crab gave love a bad name.

Lobster was living
la dolce vita.

Lobster was listening to
Michael Bublé on repeat.

Lobster had started
a dream home
Pinterest board.

Lobster felt the need
to call her to discuss
his sandwich choice.

Lobster loved
everything about her.

Lobster thought he was
just riveting.

Just one more episode,
thought Lobster and
Lobster.

Love had made Lobster
just a little bit crazy.

Lobster and Lobster
had matching
record collections.

Lobster thought
he was unstoppable
with her by his side.

Lobster had used
his best chat-up line.

Lobster and Lobster
agreed to differ.

Lobster's heart was
in the right place.

Lobster was determined to maintain an air of mystery.

Lobster thought that
embarrassment was
only temporary, but
love was eternal.

An Hachette UK Company
www.hachette.co.uk

First published in Great Britain
in 2020 by Spruce, an imprint of
Octopus Publishing Group Ltd
Carmelite House
50 Victoria Embankment
London EC4Y 0DZ
www.octopusbooks.co.uk

Distributed in the US by
Hachette Book Group
1290 Avenue of the Americas
4th and 5th Floors
New York, NY 10104

Distributed in Canada by
Canadian Manda Group
664 Annette St.
Toronto, Ontario,
Canada M6S 2C8

ISBN 978-1-84601-588-5

A CIP catalogue record for this
book is available from the British
Library.

Printed and bound in Spain

10 9 8 7 6 5 4 3 2 1

Commissioned by
Emily Brickell

Senior Editor
Alex Stetter

Designer and Illustrator
Anita Mangan

Design Assistant
Robyn Shiner

Art Director
Geoff Fennell

Production Controller
Grace O'Byrne

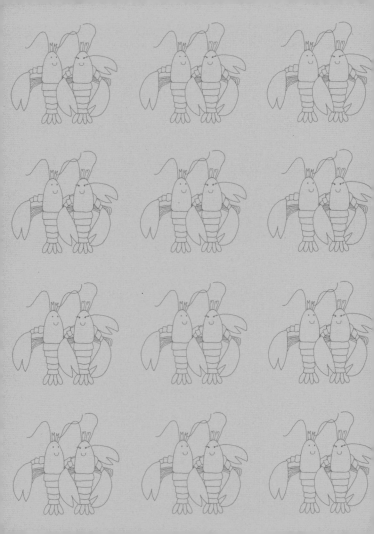

Contents

Introduction
A PATTERN TO FOLLOW ~ pages 4–5

Chapter 1
THE JEWS – A PRAYING PEOPLE ~ pages 6–11

Chapter 2
OUR FATHER ~ pages 12–19

Chapter 3
HALLOWED BE THY NAME ~ pages 20–27

Chapter 4
THY KINGDOM COME ~ pages 28–35

Chapter 5
THY WILL BE DONE ~ pages 36–41

Chapter 6
GIVE US THIS DAY OUR DAILY BREAD ~ pages 42–47

Chapter 7
FORGIVEN AND FORGIVING ~ pages 48–55

Chapter 8
THE ORDEAL OF TEMPTATION ~ pages 56–63

Epilogue ~ page 64

INTRODUCTION

A pattern to follow

Often when we had a letter to write when we were very young we would go to our parents and ask: 'What will I say?' Many of us, perhaps indeed most of us, remain like that all our lives.

When a person comes with this request, the person helping can simply dictate the letter. But that is not the best way to help. For if the help is given in that way the letter will be someone else's letter.

There is another way to help. The person needing help may be given an outline and a pattern, which will be a guide. This is far the better way, for then the person is enabled to say the right things, but to say them in his own way.

WHAT WILL I PRAY?

It is exactly this that happened with Jesus and his disciples in regard to prayer. They wanted to pray. They knew their own needs and desires; but they did not know how to set about praying.

"Lord," they said, *"teach us to pray" (Luke 11:1)*

"When you pray," said Jesus, *"pray like this,"* and he taught them the Lord's Prayer *(Luke 11:2; Matthew 6:9).*

The experience of the disciples is the experience of very many of us. We wish to pray for we know well that we need God. But we hardly know how to start; and we do not know how to put it. And Jesus gives us not only a prayer to repeat in itself, but a prayer to be for us the pattern of our own prayers.

The pattern is very simple but very comprehensive. In the Lord's Prayer Jesus says to us:

When you pray,
Remember that God is your Father and your King, and that, therefore, you go to One in whom Love and Power are equally combined.

When you pray,
Do not hesitate to tell God about your daily needs.

When you pray,
Do not shrink from telling God about your mistakes.

When you pray,
Never forget to place the unknown future and all its perils in the hands of God.

CHAPTER ONE

The Jews – a Praying People

The Jews were pre-eminently a praying people. "The Holy One," said the rabbis, "yearns for the prayers of his people." So we do well to see the Jewish heritage of prayer which the disciples learned before they ever received the teaching of Jesus.

THE GOD WHO HEARS

No Jew doubted the power of prayer. The rabbis said, "Prayer, the weapon of the mouth, that is mighty." No Jew doubted that God's ear and heart were open to the prayer of all his children.

CONSTANT PRAYER

As the Jewish teachers saw it, prayer is not so much an emergency appeal in need as it is a continuing and unbroken conversation and fellowship with God.

In a rabbinic commentary on *Isaiah 1:11 and 13*, we read, *"God said to Israel, Be assiduous in regard to devotion, for there is no finer quality than prayer. Prayer is greater than all the sacrifices."*

OUR OFFERING TO GOD

In his book, *The Jewish Religion*, Friedlander very beautifully sets out the feelings lead a man to pray. We ought to take everything that is in our hearts and lay it before God.

- ❖ We should bring our love.
- ❖ We should bring our gratitude and thanksgiving.
- ❖ Above all, we will take all our weakness to the strength of God.

FROM MIDRASH, A RABBINIC COMMENTARY

"A human king can hearken to two or three people at once, but he cannot hearken to more; God is not so, for all men may pray to him, and he hearkens to them all simultaneously. Men's ears become satisfied with hearing; but God's ears are never satiated. He is never wearied by men's prayers."

MIDRASH ON PSALM 65

"Whenever Israel knocks at the door of God's house, the Holy One rejoices."

MIDRASH ON PSALM 4

GOD'S HOLINESS

However much a man comes to God in love and in trust and in confidence, there must still be that reverence which will prevent an undue familiarity on the part of the creature before his Creator.

There must therefore be the desire to obey and to please God, and there will be the fear to offend God. It is only the person with clean hands and a pure heart who can ascend into the hill of the Lord *(Psalm 24:3, 4)*.

The heritage of prayer

There are still other things which we must note about the Jewish idea of prayer that we may see still more clearly the heritage which the disciples already possessed before Jesus taught them to pray.

PENITENCE

Even if the congregation can bring nothing else, they can weep and pray and God will receive them.

THE PRAYING COMMUNITY

The prayer of an individual always tends to be, or runs the risk of being selfish; and, therefore, the highest kind of prayer is the prayer of the community, from which a man must never separate himself.

"Even when the edge of the sword already touches a man's neck, even then he must not abandon his faith in praying to God."
THE TALMUD

"In his prayer a man should think that the Shechinah (i.e. the glory of God) is before him."
RABBI SIMON

PERSEVERANCE

Moses still prayed for the mercy of
God, even when God said to him,
"Enough for thee, speak no more to
me of this matter!"

> *"Why is the prayer of the
> righteous like a rake? As
> the rake turns the grain
> from place to place, so
> the prayer of the
> righteous turns the
> attribute of mercy."*
>
> YEB. 64A

HUMILITY

A haughty prayer is an abomination.
The Jews had a curious saying: "To three sins man is daily
liable, thought of evil, *reliance on prayer*, and slander. He
who prays thinking he deserves an answer, receives none."
There can be a confidence in prayer which is an arrogant
supposition that God must do what those who pray ask.

INTERCESSION

Intercession was specially precious. It is a prayer which is
uttered on behalf of another which is always answered first.

JEWISH PRAYER –
THE DANGERS OF FORMALISM

The Jews were so anxious to see that prayer was never
omitted that the tendency was to surround it with rules.

There were rules with regard to time (at 9am, 12noon
and 3pm), place, and length.

There were written prayers for all events of life and
some Jews said that even a slip in the correct wording
could be fatal.

A WORLD FULL OF GOD

It is easy to see how the custom and ritual of set prayers
might well become little more than a kind of use of
magic incantations, but surely it is equally easy to see how

a man who had such habits of prayer necessarily lived in a world which was full of God, a world in which there were no events which did not turn his heart to the Creator and the Sustainer of all life.

KAWANNAH

Formalism was abhorrent to the devout Jew. The first necessity of prayer is *kawannah* - concentrated intention and devotion.

Great Jewish Prayers

We may conclude our examination of the Jewish ideas of prayer by choosing out of very many, two great Jewish prayers, which the Jews still pray and which any Christian might pray with profit.

A PRAYER BEFORE SLEEPING

Blessed art thou, O Lord our God, King of the Universe, who makest the hands of sleep to fall upon mine eyes, and slumber upon mine eyelids. May it be thy will, O Lord my God, and God of my fathers, to suffer me to lie down in peace and to let me rise again in peace. Let not my thoughts trouble me, nor evil dreams, nor evil fancies, but let my rest be perfect before thee. O lighten mine eyes lest I sleep the sleep of death, for it is thou who givest light to the apple of the eye. Blessed art thou, O Lord, who givest light to the whole world in thy glory.

THE PRAYER OF RAB:

May it be thy will, O Lord our God, to grant us long life, a life of peace, a life of good, a life of blessing, a life of sustenance, a life of bodily vigor, a life marked by the fear of sin, a life free from shame and reproach, a life of prosperity and honor, and a life in which love of the Law and fear of heaven shall cling to us, a life wherein thou fulfillest the desire of the heart for good.

OTHER JEWISH PRAYERS

PRAYER AT THE SIGHT OF FRUITS, OR WINE OR VEGETABLES:

"Blessed art thou who createst the fruit of the tree, the fruit of the vine, the fruit of the earth."

PRAYER UPON SEEING SHOOTING STARS, EARTHQUAKES, LIGHTNINGS, THUNDERS AND STORMS:

"Blessed is he whose power and might fill the world."

PRAYER UPON SEEING MOUNTAINS, HILLS, RIVERS, DESERTS:

"Blessed is the author of creation."

AT BAD TIDINGS:

"Blessed is he, the true judge."

CHAPTER TWO

Our Father

Two Meanings

The word father has two quite distinct meanings.

I Paternity

It can be used in the sense of *paternity*. In that sense it simply denotes the person who is responsible for the birth of a child. In that case there is no necessary connection between the father and the child other than a physical connection.

II Fatherhood

The word father can be used in the sense of *fatherhood*. In that sense it describes a relationship of love and intimacy and confidence and trust between the father and the child.

PATERNITY AND FATHERHOOD

The Christian believes that God is father in the paternity sense of the word, in the sense that it is God who is the source of all life, who gives life to any child.

But the unique thing about the Christian idea of God is the belief that God is father in the fatherhood sense of the word, that between God and man, there is possible through Jesus Christ, an intimate, lifelong, loving relationship in which God and man come closer together. This is indeed a distinction which the Jewish teachers themselves made.

AN OLD JEWISH STORY

The rabbis told a story of an orphan girl who was brought up by a good and faithful guardian. When the time came for her marriage, the Scribe who was making the legal arrangements asked her, "What is your name?"

And she told him. Then the Scribe asked: "What is your father's name?"

The girl was silent. "Why are you silent?" asked her guardian.

"Because I know none other than you as a father, for he who brings up is father, not he who begets."

So, the rabbis said, the real father of Israel is not anyone who is connected with Israel by any physical connection; it is God who brought the nation up.

> ### JEWISH SAYINGS
>
> *"You are the sons of the Lord your God."*
> DEUTERONOMY 14:1
>
> *"I am a father to Israel."*
> JEREMIAH 31:9

A RICH HERITAGE

When Jesus taught his disciples to pray, Our Father, he was speaking out of a rich heritage. For the fatherhood of God was a conception that was supremely dear to a Jew.

Two Assurances

Their conviction of the fatherhood of God brought certain assurances to the Jews.

I The nearness of God

Their belief in the fatherhood of God assured them of *the nearness of God*.

Because God is father, the Jewish saints were sure that God is always near to hear and to answer prayer and to give his presence to his people.

THE SHECHINAH

The *Shechinah* was the glory of God. It sometimes settled on the Tabernacle and on the Temple in a luminous cloud.

When God said to Moses, "Make me a dwelling-place," Moses wondered. For Moses knew that the glory of God fills the world and he could not understand how the glory of God could dwell in a dwelling-place that he might be able to construct.

II The mercy of God

The belief of the Jews in the fatherhood of God assured them of the mercy of God in judgement. God was willing to accept the penitent heart.

Very beautifully it was said: "God says to Israel: For all the wonders and mighty deeds which I have wrought for you, the only reward I ask is that

---

ONE SQUARE YARD

But God can confine his glory to one square yard.

Just because God is Father and we are his children: in the humblest home, even in the littlest and barest church, even for the most unimportant person, the glory of God is there. Anywhere the Father can be and will be with his children.

you should honor me as my children, and call me your Father." *R. Mishpatim*

The essence of God's relationship to men is fatherhood, and the dearest wish of God is that all his children should willingly enter into that relationship.

JUDGEMENT DAY FOR TWO MEN

The Jewish saints thought of God as judge, but they thought of him as a judge who was also a father.

There is a Jewish passage which tells of two men who came to the judgement seat in terror of the judge and who were told to take courage. The angels said to them,

"Fear not! Do you not recognize the Judge?
He is your fellow-citizen, see *Isaiah 45:13;*
he is your relative, see *Psalm 148:14;*
he is your brother, see *Psalm 122:8;*
and even more, he is your Father, see
Deuteronomy 32:6."

Here is the beautiful thought that he who is judge is also fellow-citizen, relative, brother, and above all Father.

Two Responsibilities

In spite of the beauty of the Jewish idea of the fatherhood of God, the Jews never sentimentalized the idea.

I Obedience

The Jews were quite clear that the fatherhood of God involves the loving obedience of man. They were very definite that the idea of God as a loving father can never be used as an excuse for sinning; it must rather be the summons to holy obedience.

"MY CHILDREN ... NOT MY CHILDREN"

When the prophets prayed to God to have mercy on his children, God answered: "Only when they do my will are they my children; when they do not do my will they are not my children." *Exodus R. Ki Tissa xlvi, 4*

THE BATTLE WITH AMALEK

The Jewish saints allegorized the incident in *Exodus 17:11.* It tells how in the battle with Amalek Israel prevailed, as long as Moses held up his hands, but was defeated when Moses let his hands drop.

"But could the hands of Moses promote the battle or hinder the battle? It is rather to teach you that such time as the Israelites directed their thoughts on high, and kept their hearts in subjection to their Father in heaven, they prevailed; otherwise they suffered defeat."
Rosh ha-Shanah 3.8

II Brotherhood

The thought of the fatherhood of God laid upon the Jew the obligation to observe the brotherhood of man.

Rabbi Jose said, "Why does God love widows and orphans? Because their eyes are turned to him, as it is said, A father of the fatherless, and a judge of the widows, see *Psalm 68:5.* Therefore, anyone who robs them is as if he robbed God, their Father in heaven."

If God is Father, than God will never look lightly on the man who injures or refuses to help one of his children.

DOING THE WILL OF THE FATHER

The duty of the teacher of children is to teach children "to do the will of their Father who is in heaven." Rabbi Judah gave this beautiful command:

"Be strong as a leopard, light as an eagle, fleet as a hart, and strong as a lion to do the will of thy Father who is in heaven."
ABOTH V.23

The Jews always connected the thought of the loving and gracious fatherhood of God not with any kind of licence to sin, but with the absolute obligation to the response of loving obedience.

Abba

Great as the word father is, at first sight, to apply this word to God, is still greater when we penetrate further into its meaning.

ABBA IN THE NEW TESTAMENT

In Gethsemane Jesus prayed, *"Abba, Father." Mark 14:36* Paul twice writes that we through the Holy Spirit can pray in the same way, and that we can use the same word as Jesus did when we, too, pray to God. See *Romans 8:15; Galatians 4:6.*

MORE THAN FATHER

This word abba is more than father. It was the word by which a little child in Palestine addressed his father in the home circle, There is only one possible English translation of this word in any ordinary use of it, and that is "Daddy".

"DADDY"

Of course, to translate it that way in the New Testament would sound bizarre and grotesque, but it does at once give us the atmosphere in which we come to God. We come to God with the simple trust and confidence with which a little child comes to a father whom he knows and loves and trusts.

JEREMIAS

Jeremias points out that there is no parallel in the whole of Jewish literature for the application of this word to God.

OUR RELATIONSHIP TO GOD

It settles once and for all our relationship to God. This is the spirit, this is the confidence, this is the intimacy with which we come to God.

When we go to Jesus' own words, we can still further fill out the meaning of this word.

I God cares
First and foremost, it tells us that God cares. So far from being isolated, detached, insulated against all emotion, God cares for all men with the constant love of a father, and with such a passion of love that in the end, in Jesus Christ, he suffered the agony of the Cross.

II A quite undeserved love
This love of God is a quite undeserved love. Jesus cites as typical of this fatherly love of God that God makes his sun to rise on the evil and the good and sends his rain on the just and the unjust. *Matthew 5:45.*

III A practical love
This fatherly love of God is a practical love. It knows well that we need food and clothing and all the necessary things of life. Our Father knows that we need these things. See *Matthew 6:8, 31; Luke 12:30.*

We can pray to God for our practical, worrying, everyday needs. There is nothing which we cannot take to God in prayer.

CHAPTER THREE

Hallowed be Thy Name

Name

We turn to the definition of the meaning of the words in this petition with the meaning of the word *name*.

NAME MANIFESTS CHARACTER

In biblical times the *name* stood for much more than the name by which a person is called in the modern sense of the term. The name stood for the whole character of the person as it was known, manifested or revealed.

ORIGEN

As Origen puts in, commenting on this petition of the Lord's Prayer, "Name is a term which summarizes and manifests the personal character of him who is named." The name stands for "the personal and incommunicable character" of the person.

The *name* of God, therefore, stands for the nature and the character of the personality of God as they have been revealed to men.

Hallow

We now examine the meaning of
the word *hallow*.

TO HOLD SACRED

In Greek the word is *hagiazein*. In
biblical Greek this word means to treat
as holy, that is *to hold sacred*.

To hallow a thing is to regard and to
treat that thing as holy and sacred.

THE IDEA OF DIFFERENCE

What does it mean to hold something
as sacred? We can best come at this
from remembering the meaning of
hagios. *Hagios* is the adjective meaning
holy; but the basic idea behind it is the idea of difference.

That which is *hagios* is different from ordinary things;
it belongs to a different sphere of quality and of being.
That is why God is supremely The Holy One, for God
supremely belongs to a different sphere of life and being.

THE SABBATH DAY

This meaning becomes even clearer when we examine
the word in use. The commandment is to remember the
Sabbath day to keep it *holy*. *Exodus 20:8*. That is to say, the
Sabbath day is to be regarded and to be kept as different
from other days.

REVERENCE

We can now see that the meaning of the word *hagiazein* is
beginning to acquire the meaning of *reverence*.

> ### WHAT GOD IS LIKE
>
> *In John 17:6 Jesus says,*
>
> **"I have manifested thy
> name to the men whom
> thou gavest me out of the
> world."**
>
> *In effect, that means that
> Jesus clearly told his own
> what God is like, what the
> nature and the character
> and the personality of God
> truly are. The name can
> stand for nothing less than
> God himself.*

21

AN OLD TESTAMENT ILLUSTRATION

There is an Old Testament passage, *Numbers 20:1-11*, which well illustrates the meaning of this word *hagiazein*.

SPEAK TO THE ROCK

The story is that the children of Israel in their journeys in the wilderness were near to perishing of thirst, and were full of bitter complaints. God instructs Moses to take his rod and to *speak* to the rock and to tell the rock to give forth water.

MOSES STRIKES THE ROCK

But Moses, instead of only speaking to the rock, in his anger and irritation *struck* the rock. Then there comes this statement:

"Because you did not believe in me to *sanctify* me in the eyes of the people of Israel you shall not bring this assembly into the land which I have given them."

IRREVERENCE

The verb to sanctify is *hagiazein*. Moffatt translates it, "because you did not vindicate my honor", and the Smith-Goodspeed translation is, "because you did not pay me my due honor".

Basically, the idea is that the action of Moses was an action of *irreverence* in that it implied disobedience to, and distrust of God. By taking the law into his own hands, Moses had been guilty of irreverence towards God.

> *Reverence is the characteristic attitude to that which is different, that which belongs to a sphere of being other than our own.*

TO HALLOW MEANS TO REVERENCE

So we arrive at the conclusion that to *hallow* means to *reverence*.

Reverence

REVERENCE IN THE LORD'S PRAYER

To hallow is to hold in reverence. If we, then, pray, "Hallowed be thy name", the prayer means, "May you be given that unique reverence which your character and nature and personality, as you have revealed them to us, demand."

The prayer is that God may be given that reverence which his divine being demands and necessitates, and which, through his self-revelation, we well know to be due to him.

REVERENCE IN 1 PETER

We get exactly the same idea in regard to Jesus in *1 Peter 3:15* where Peter bids his people, "Reverence (*hagiazein*) Christ as Lord." To Jesus there must be given the reverence which his lordship demands.

To hallow God's name is to give God the reverence, the honor, the glory, the praise, the exaltation which his character demands.

JOHN CALVIN

Calvin put it this way,

"That God's name should be hallowed is nothing other than to say that God should have his own honor, of which he is worthy, so that men should never think or speak of him without the greatest veneration."

THE DANGER OF SENTIMENTALIZATION

No doctrine is more liable to be sentimentalized than the doctrine of the fatherhood of God. But any sentimentalization for a Jew is essentially impossible. For a Jew God is The Wholly Other; no Jew could ever think of God without reverence.

HOW TO REVERENCE GOD

I Our beliefs

We reverence God *when our beliefs concerning God are such as are worthy of God*. That is to say that true doctrine and true teaching are reverence for God. False doctrine and false teaching are irreverence to God.

ORIGEN'S TEACHING

Origen's teaching on prayer brings this out.
"God has revealed himself as 'He who is'. *Exodus 3:14*. Now everyone makes his own suppositions about God; everyone knows something about God; but man being man can only grasp a very little of the holiness of God. And, because we are liable to make mistakes, and to confuse partial truths with the whole truth, we are taught to pray 'that our concept of God may be hallowed among us.' ORIGEN.

"The man who brings into his concept of God ideas which have no place there takes the name of the Lord God in vain." ORIGEN.

FAILURE TO HALLOW GOD

Since the *name* of God means *the nature and the character of God*, anyone who brings into his idea of God thoughts and conceptions which are alien to the true character of God is guilty of irreverence and of failure to hallow the name of God.

CHRISTIANS ARE NOT GUILTLESS

But Christians themselves have been far from guiltless in this matter.

> ### THE GREEKS AND THEIR GODS
>
> *To take the obvious example, the Greeks with their stories of the wars and battles and struggles and quarrels, the loves and hates and seductions and adulteries of the gods, were in fact guilty of irreverence, for they were bringing into the conception of God things which had no right to be there.*

- ❖ Very often men have been repelled by ideas of God which show God as savage, vindictive, harsh and cruel, and the very opposite of the God whom we see in Jesus Christ.
- ❖ There have been times when God has been presented as a God of battles and a kind of nationalistic ally.
- ❖ There have been times when men have drawn a picture of God to suit their own theories of racial superiority.
- ❖ There have been times when men used their own ideas of God to erect a barrier to all social progress, and when they did indeed make religion the opiate of the people, when they made religion an argument for maintaining the *status quo*.

25

**DISHONORING
GOD'S NAME**

*To allow into our
conception of God things
which are unworthy of
God, and things which
can have no place in the
God who is the God and
Father of our Lord Jesus
Christ is to fail to hallow
the name of God.*

John Wesley was right when he said
of one who had warped beliefs about
God: "Your God is my devil."

II Our behavior

We reverence God and we hallow God's name, *when our
life is such that it brings honor to God and attracts others to him.*
This is an idea to which the early fathers return again
and again.

I CYRIL OF JERUSALEM

Cyril of Jerusalem *(Catechetical Lecture 23)* begins by saying
that quite clearly God's name is in itself and in its nature
holy, no matter what we may say or do, or not say or not
do. The prayer cannot possibly mean that God's name
should become holy from not being holy.

We are to pray this prayer because God's name
"becomes holy in us, when we are made holy, and do
things worthy of holiness."

II CYPRIAN

Cyprian *(On the Lord's Prayer 12)* says that it is obviously
impossible that we should wish for God that he should be
hallowed by our prayer; what we do ask is that "his name
should be hallowed in us."

III TERTULLIAN

Tertullian *(On Prayer 3)* says exactly the same thing. The prayer is that "God's name may be hallowed in us."

IV AUGUSTINE

Augustine *(The Sermon on the Mount 5.19)* makes the same point. It is not that God's name is not already holy. What we do pray for is that men should regard it as holy, that is to say, that God may become so near and dear to us that we will esteem nothing more holy than his name and dread nothing more than to offend it.

ENTHRONE GOD

If we are to hallow the name of God we must first of all enthrone God within our hearts.

PSALM 30

Origen quotes *Psalm 30:1*: "I will extol thee, O Lord, for thou hast drawn me up, and hast not let my foes rejoice over me." In this Psalm the Psalmist extols, hallows, the name of God.

Origen then quotes the title of *Psalm 30*: "A Psalm of David. A song at the dedication of the Temple." Then he draws this deduction: "We extol God when we dedicate within ourselves a house to God."

> ### MARTIN LUTHER
>
> Luther asks:"How is it [God's name] hallowed among us?"
> And he gives the answer:
> "When our life and doctrine are truly Christian."

A TEMPLE IN OUR HEARTS

To extol God, to hallow God's name, must mean that we make our hearts his temple and his dwelling-place, for only when he dwells within our hearts will our lives truly honor him and truly draw others to him.

CHAPTER FOUR

Thy Kingdom Come

Two general facts

It would be both possible and natural to hold that "Thy Kingdom come" is the central petition of the Lord's Prayer. For it is certain that the Kingdom of God was the central message and proclamation of Jesus.

THE CENTRALITY OF THE KINGDOM

The announcement of the Kingdom was the purpose for which Jesus came into the world. The centrality of the idea of the Kingdom is made clear from the fact that the phrase the Kingdom of God, or the Kingdom of Heaven appears 49 times in Matthew, 16 times in Mark and 38 times in Luke.

I The kingship or reign of God

This is the first general fact to note. It might be better to talk of the *kingship* or of the *reign* of God. Nowadays the word kingdom suggests a certain territory such as the kingdom of Belgium or the kingdom of Holland.

NOT A TERRITORY, A REIGN

But in the New Testament the kingdom is not a territory; it is the reign of God.

"The Kingdom of God is at hand" means "God is on the point of beginning his reign; the kingship, the royal power, of God within the world, is about to begin."

II The Kingdom of God or the Kingdom of Heaven?

This is the second general point. The New Testament uses two phrases, the Kingdom of God and the Kingdom of Heaven which mean exactly the same. It is an error to try to make any distinction between them.

MATTHEW, MARK AND LUKE

Matthew hardly ever speaks of the Kingdom of God and practically always speaks of the Kingdom of Heaven. Mark and Luke hardly ever use the Kingdom of Heaven – almost always the Kingdom of God. Why the difference? The reason is this. A devout Jew avoided using the name of God at all. If possible he used some reverential periphrasis such as heaven, which is what Matthew, the most Jeish of the writers, does, while Mark and Luke, much less influenced by Jewish background, do not hesitate to speak of the Kingdom of God.

Characteristics of the Kingdom

I An invitation

It is entirely natural that the Kingdom of God should *begin with an invitation*. It begins with the personal invitation of God to every man to accept his will, as that will is known in Jesus Christ.

A BANQUET

It may therefore be pictured as a feast and a banquet to which the host issues invitations, which the guests can accept or refuse to their glory or their shame *(Matthew 22:1-14; Luke 14:16-24)*.

To enter the Kingdom is to accept the invitation of God to be his guest, and a guest must always accept the laws and rules of the family into which he enters.

II Repentance

That is why *the Kingdom of God and repentance go hand in hand*. The initial message of Jesus was a summons to repent because God was about to begin his reign *(Mark 1:14; Matthew 4:17)*.

The instinctive human relationship to life is to make our own will, wishes and desires the dominating and moving force in life. When a man enters the Kingdom he has that change of mind which makes him stop obeying his own will and begin accepting God's will, which makes him

---

METANOIA

Repentance is literally a change of mind (metanoia); and conversion is literally a turning round and facing in the opposite direction.

stop looking at himself and start looking at God.

III The smallest beginning

This is why the Kingdom of God necessarily starts from the smallest beginnings. People do not enter the Kingdom in crowds; they must enter as individuals; for the moment of entry is the personal and individual acceptance of the will of God.

THE MUSTARD SEED

That is why the growth of the mustard seed, the smallest of all seeds, into a tree symbolizes the Kingdom *(Matthew 13:31,32)*.

That is why, if a person is placed in an environment which is hostile or indifferent to the claims of God, he must not regard it as something to regret or resent, but as a privilege and a challenge to be the tiny seed from which the Kingdom grows.

> ### THE JEWISH VIEW
>
> *The Jews saw the Kingdom in terms of*
> * *material prosperity*
> * *political power*
> * *national greatness.*

IV The difference

Jesus' Kingdom is different from earthly kingdoms. "My kingship," said Jesus to Pilate, "is not of this world." *(John 18:36)*

In the Kingdom of God the Jews expected at last to take their place in world leadership.

AN INNER KINGDOM

But Jesus said, "My kingdom is within (or among) you." *(Luke 17:21)* The Kingdom must come in the hearts of men before the Kingdom could even begin to come in the world at large.

Entering the Kingdom

I Worth the effort

To enter the kingdom of God is *worth the effort*. Jesus said: "Seek first his Kingdom and his righteousness." *(Matthew 6:33)* This has been well translated: "Make the Kingdom of God the object of all your endeavor."

IN EARNEST

The Kingdom is for those for those who are desperately in earnest. Quite simply the meaning is:

❖ It is worth the effort.
❖ It is worth the agony.
❖ It is worth any blood and sweat and tears to do the will of God, and therefore to be a citizen and member of the Kingdom.

II At any price

The Kingdom of God is worth *any price*.

THE TREASURE AND THE PEARL

Jesus told the twin parables of the treasure hid in the field and the pearl of great price *(Matthew 13:44-46)*. In both cases the discoverer of the treasure gave his all to become the possessor of the treasure.

It may well be that in order to become a member of the Kingdom and in order to do the will of God a man may have to pay a costly price.

❖ He may have to sacrifice his ease and comfort that he might have enjoyed.
❖ He may have to lay aside a personal ambition which he might well have attained.

❖ He may have to sacrifice even the nearest and
dearest personal relationships, for Jesus demanded
that loyalty to him should exceed even the loyalties
to kith and kin which are at the very heart of
human life. *(Matthew 10:37; Luke 14:26)*

The meaning is that there is no price too high to pay
to be a member of the Kingdom and to do the will of God.

III Any sacrifice

To enter the Kingdom of God is worth *any sacrifice*.

The hand, the eye, the foot, which are liable to
become a cause of sin have to be torn out and to cut off
and thrown away *(Matthew 10:29, 30)*. No sacrifice is too
radical if it is the price of entering the Kingdom.

GOD IS NO MAN'S DEBTOR

In this matter God will be in no man's debt. If the battle
is bitter, the reward of victory is great. Whatever sacrifice a
man makes, it will be repaid him a hundredfold *(Luke
18:29; Mark 10:28-30; Matthew 19:27-30)*.

The struggle is not for nothing and therefore it can be
faced with gallantry and joy.

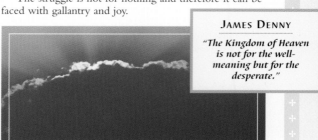

> ### JAMES DENNY
>
> *"The Kingdom of Heaven
> is not for the well-
> meaning but for the
> desperate."*

Barriers to the Kingdom

There are certain barriers to entry to the Kingdom

I Lip service

Lip service debars a man from entry to the Kingdom. It is not the man who says "Lord, Lord," who will enter the Kingdom but the man who does the will of God *(Matthew 7:21)*.

Profession without practice is maybe one of the commonest faults within the Church.

II The unforgiving spirit

The unforgiving spirit debars a man from the Kingdom. Jesus makes this quite clear in the parable of the unforgiving debtor *(Matthew 18:23-35)*.

❖ A merciless man can have no fellowship with the merciful God.

❖ A heart of hatred has automatically shut itself to the love of God.

❖ A man who will not forgive cannot enter into the presence of the God whose one desire is to forgive.

There is no place in the Kingdom for any man who in his heart nourishes a grudge against a fellowman and who in his life has an unhealed breach between himself and another.

III Riches

Riches make entry into the Kingdom very difficult. Jesus said, "Truly I say to you, it will be hard for a rich man to enter the Kingdom of Heaven. Again I tell you, it is easier for a camel to go through the eye of a needle than for a rich man to enter the Kingdom of God" *(Matthew 9:23, 24; Mark 10:23-27; Luke 18:24, 25).*

> ### Dr Johnson
>
> *Dr Johnson made his famous remark to Boswell after leaving the castle of a great nobleman:*
>
> **"Ah, Boswell, these are the things which make it difficult to die."**

Why? There are two main reasons.

a. Possessions fix us to this world

First, the possession of many material things tend to fix a man's interests and thoughts to this world. He has so large a stake in this world that he can scarcely lift his eyes beyond it.

It is possible for a man to get so involved in this world that he forgets that there is any other.

b. Riches can be "a rival salvation"

Second, riches can become what someone has called "a rival salvation".

- ❖ They give a false sense of security.
- ❖ They tend to make a man think that he can buy his way into and out of anything.
- ❖ They tend to make a man think that he can cope very well with life himself, and to make him forget God.

Conclusion

No man need pray this prayer, "Thy Kingdom come", unless he is prepared to hand himself over to the grace of God in order that that grace may make him a new creature.

CHAPTER FIVE

Thy Will be Done

Different meanings

It might well be said that "Thy will be done" is not only one of the petitions that Jesus taught his disciples to pray, but that it is also the center, the key-note, and the ruling principle of Jesus' own life.

Especially in the Fourth Gospel Jesus is represented as the One who came into the world for no other purpose than to do the will of God.

TONE OF VOICE

This petition, "Thy will be done", can mean very different things; the tone of voice in which it is spoken, and the emotion which gave it birth make all the difference.

I Bitter resentment

It can be spoken in *bitter resentment*. It can be the statement of one who knows that there is no escape and that there is no other way, but who is filled with rebellious, angry, bitter resentment that it should be so.

BEETHOVEN

Life was hard for Beethoven. In particular, it was a terrible fate for one whose very soul was music that he should have to experience complete deafness. It is said that when they found him dead, his fists were clenched, as if he would strike God, and his lips were drawn back in a snarl, as if he would spit his defiance and his bitterness at God.

There are many people who know quite well that they must accept the will of God, but who spend their life in bitter resentment that it should be so.

II Resignation

It can be spoken in the tone of one who *resignedly accepts a situation, not so much in bitterness, as because there is nothing else to do but to admit defeat.*

EMPEROR JULIAN

Julian was the Roman Emperor who tried to put the clock back. He tried to reverse the decision of Constantine that Christianity should be the religion of the Empire, and reintroduce the worship of the ancient gods. In the end he was mortally wounded in battle in the east.

When he lay bleeding to death, he took a handful of his blood and tossed it in the air, saying: "You have conquered, O man of Galilee!" It is not so much that he submitted; it was rather that he wearily accepted defeat, because there was nothing else to do.

III Grudging acceptance

It can be spoken in the tone of voice of one who in the end accepts something, not exactly in weary resignation, but in the conviction that he cannot in any event do anything about it, the tone of voice of one who yields with a more or less good grace to *force majeure*.

> ### A GRAY ACCEPTANCE
>
> *There is indeed an acceptance of the will of God which can be completely joyless. It is tired and weary and defeated and resigned, not content, still less glad, but only resigned to the fact that things must be so. There are many who live in a gray acceptance that things are as they are.*

REINHOLD NIEBUHR'S DAUGHTER

Niebuhr loved to tell a story about how he wanted his daughter to come out for a walk, but she did not want to go. He extolled the virtues of exercise and fresh air, and in the end she came. As they ended their walk, he turned to her and said: "Now aren't you glad that you decided to come?"

To this his daughter replied: "I didn't decide. You were just bigger!" Her philosophy was that it was better to do without a struggle what in the end you would be compelled to do anyway! There are some people who accept the will of God just because God is "bigger".

JOYLESS

They are not particularly resentful; and they are not particularly defeated and resigned; but equally they have no thrill and throb of joy in making God's will their choice. They could never say "Oh, how I *love* thy law!"

IV Trustful love

It can be spoken in a tone of *serene and trustful love and joy and peace*. It can be spoken in the tone of one who is quite sure that "a father's hand will never cause his child a needless tear".

RICHARD CAMERON

In the days of the Covenanters terrible things happened in Scotland, as the government by the most savage measures tried to crush the Covenanters out of existence. Richard Cameron was one of the most famous and one of the greatest of them. They captured Richard Cameron's son.

The son had notably beautiful hands. They cut off the hands and sent them to the father with a kind of wanton cruelty.

Richard Cameron recognized them at once. "They are my son's," he said, "my own dear son's. It is the Lord's will and good is the will of the Lord. He has never wronged me or mine."

COMPLETE ACCEPTANCE

Here is the complete and trusting acceptance of anything that might or could happen, as part of the will of God. Here is neither resentment, nor defeatedness; here there is the determination never to doubt the will of God.

What is God really like?

We need to remind ourselves again and again what God is really like. There are two things in God which, if we really believe them, should make it easy to pray this prayer.

I The wisdom of God

We believe in the wisdom of God. We believe that God in his wisdom knows far better than we do what is for our ultimate good.

GOD AND TIME

We believe that only God sees all time. In the nature of things we must live in the moment. The past is past and cannot be recalled; we cannot see even a moment ahead. God alone can see the whole pattern of life, and therefore, God alone can see what is our ultimate good.

II The love of God

We believe in the *love* of God. Now it is just here that we part company with the Stoics. The Stoics believed that literally everything is in accordance with the will of God. The Stoic went on to say that a man must teach himself not to care what happened to anyone or to himself or to anything he had, because whatever happened was the will of God.

BLASPHEMOUS USE OF "GOD'S WILL"

Nothing has done the Christian faith and the Church more harm than the indiscriminate and blasphemous use of the phrase, "It is God's will". It is a blasphemous slander on God to attribute to him acts and situations and events which, if we believe in the love of God in Jesus Christ, are the exact opposite of his will.

CONCLUSION

We can only lovingly obey God when we receive Jesus Christ into our hearts. Then he will give us the dynamic to say, as he himself said, "Thy will be done."

THE STOICS

Long before Christianity entered this world the Stoics held this point of view. They held, not that God is Eimarmente, Fate, but that God is Pronoia, Providence. The Stoics could, therefore, say the noblest things.

"I have trained myself," said Seneca, "not merely to obey God, but to agree with his decisions. I follow him because my soul wills it, and not because I must"

(LETTERS 96.2).

"Use me henceforth for whatever thou wilt," prayed Epictetus. "I have submitted my freedom of choice to God. What he does not will I do not wish"

(DISCOURSES 4.1.89).

If the heathen can say this, if a man can say this who knows nothing of God in Jesus Christ, how much more should a Christian be able to say it?

We may begin by making it our rule to always remember the perfect wisdom of God.

CHAPTER SIX

Give Us This Day Our Daily Bread

I A sacrament

This petition has been taken as a prayer for "the Sacrament of Christ's Body which we receive daily" (Augustine, *The Sermon on the Mount 2.7.25*). Augustine thought that the Communion should be received daily. He said to the newly baptized members of his congregation: "You should realize that what you have received, what you will receive in the future, you ought to receive daily."

So, if that meaning is taken, then this is a prayer for the bread of the Sacrament taken in daily Communion with Christ.

II Spiritual food

It has been taken as a prayer for spiritual food, for the
word of God in Scripture. As Augustine says, it is a prayer
for "spiritual food, namely, the divine precepts which we
are to think over and to put into practice each day". As
the hymn has it:

> *Break thou the bread of life, Dear Lord, to me,*
> *As thou didst break the loaves Beside the sea;*
> *Beyond the sacred page I seek thee, Lord,*
> *My spirit pants for thee, O living word.*

III Christ himself

This brings us to the view that this is a prayer for nothing
other than Christ himself. "I am the Bread of Life," Jesus
said. "He who comes to me shall never hunger, and he
who believes in me shall never thirst" (*John 6:35*).

Consider Matthew Arnold's poem *East London*:

> *'Twas August, and the fierce sun overhead*
> *Smote on the squalid streets of Bethnal Green,*
> *And the pale weaver, through his windows seen*
> *In Spitalfields, look'd thrice dispirited.*
> *I met a preacher there I knew, and said:*
> *"Ill and o'er-worked, how fare you in this scene?"*
> *"Bravely!" said he; "for I of late have been*
> *Much cheer'd by thoughts of Christ, The living bread."*

IV Daily bread

All these meanings may be in this petition. But it may be
much simpler if we believe that it is just what it says, a
petition for daily bread, for the simple, ordinary things
needed to keep body and soul together.

What flows from this

If we take this petition in that simple sense, certain things emerge from it.

I Us, Our

We must note right at the beginning that we are taught to pray, not, Give *me my* daily bread, but, Give *us our* daily bread. "A man," runs the Jewish saying, "should always join himself with the community in his prayers." The very use of the plural precludes all selfishness in prayer.

OUR UNCARING SOCIETY

One of the most tragic features of present day society is what one can only call an essential mutual disregard. It is a characteristic of our age that one section of the community does not care what happens to another section of society.

But the person who in praying this petition thinks only of his bread has no real conception of what the petition means.

> **J.H. NEWMAN**
>
> *"I do not ask to see The distant scene, one step enough for me."*

II Daily

The prayer is for our *daily* bread. It does not look fearfully into the distant future; it is content to take the present and to leave it in the hands of God. "Don't worry about tomorrow," Jesus said *(Matthew 6:34)*. Take a day at a time.

GREGORY OF NYSSA

Gregory of Nyssa commenting on this passage says *(The Lord's Prayer, Sermon 4)*: "God says to you as it were: He who gives you the day will give you also the things necessary for the day." He goes on: "Who causes the sun to rise? Who makes the darkness of the night to disappear? Who shows you the ray of light? Who revolves the sky so that the source of light is above the earth?

Does he who gives you so great things need your help to supply for the needs of your body?"

This is a petition which no man can pray, unless he is prepared to live a day at a time.

In this prayer a man takes his moment, which is all he has, and rests it in the goodness and the mercy and the bounty of God.

III Bread

The truly Christian person does not pray for luxuries; what he prays for is the simple food which is enough for life.

> ## MARCUS AURELIUS
>
> *All that a man possesses is:*
>
> **the instant of time in which at the very moment he is; the past is past and cannot be recalled; the future is necessarily unknown.**

GREGORY OF NYSSA

"So we say to God: Give us bread.

❖ Not delicacies or riches, nor magnificent purple robes, golden ornaments or precious stones.

❖ Nor do we ask him for landed estates, or military commands, or political leadership.

❖ We pray neither for herds of horses and oxen or other cattle in great numbers, nor for a host of slaves.

❖ We do not say, give us a prominent position in assemblies or monuments and statues raised to us, nor silken robes and musicians at meals, nor any other thing by which the soul is estranged from the thought of God and higher things; no — but only bread!"

LUXURIES OR NECESSITIES?

We do not pray for luxuries in order that "the stomach, this perpetual tax collector, may live daintily through all this." Gregory of Nyssa continues with this advice: "Cling only to what is necessary."

Immediately we go beyond that, desire and covetousness creep into life, and life is distracted and distressed. Immediately we want more than our neighbor and set our own luxury in the forefront life goes wrong.

The prayer is for the satisfaction of simple need, not for the service of selfish luxury.

IV Give

There can be Bible passages which better illustrate the meaning of the word *Give* than this passage does.

OUR PART

Jesus taught us to pray, *Give us this day our daily bread*; but if we prayed this petition and then simply sat down with folded hands and waited, we would quite certainly starve.

- ❖ The food is not going to appear all ready-made on our tables.
- ❖ God is not going to spoon feed any man.
- ❖ Prayer is never the easy way to get God to do for us what we can well do, and must certainly do for ourselves.

GOD'S PART

What this prayer does teach is that apart from and without God there would be no such things as food at all. It is God alone who has the secret of life, and God alone who has the gift of making living things. This petition acknowledges in full man's dependence on God and man's debt to God.

CONCLUSION

To pray, *Give us this day our daily bread*, is at one and the same time to express our dependence on God, our trust in God, and to challenge ourselves to the effort and the toil which will bring the gifts of God to ourselves, and through us to our fellowmen.

CHAPTER SEVEN

Forgiven and Forgiving

The universality of sin

Forgive us our debts, as we forgive our debtors *(Matthew 6:12 AV)*. It has been well pointed out that the position of this petition in the Lord's Prayer is peculiarly appropriate.

As Plummer points out:

❖ *Forgiving* follows immediately on the heels of *giving*.

❖ The previous petition asked God to give us our daily bread.

❖ This petition asks him *to forgive* us our sins.

Tertullian says: "It is fitting that after contemplating the liberality of God we should likewise address his clemency" *(On Prayer 7)*. It is the more fitting in that when we remember the richness of God's mercy we are all the more shamed by how little we deserve it.

"Forgive us our debts"

"Pray then like this," said Jesus; and one of the things which we are to pray is, "Forgive us our debts", Jesus bade all men to pray that prayer without distinction. He did not say that this is the prayer which sinners ought to pray; he said that this is the prayer that all men ought to pray.

LUTHER AND TERTULLIAN

This is proof of the universality of sin. Luther said: "we must note how here again the indigence of our miserable life is indicated; we are in the land of debts, we are up to the ears in sin."

To ask forgiveness for sin is in itself a confession of sin. Tertullian said, "A petition for pardon is itself a full confession, because he who begs for pardon fully admits his guilt".

The very constitution of man makes him a sinner. Any man who honestly faces the human situation cannot be other than conscious of his debt, and of his need to pray to be forgiven.

CONSCIOUSNESS OF SIN

The Bible is never afraid to show great men under the consciousness of sin.

Peter cried out to Jesus,

"Depart from me, for I am a sinful man."

(LUKE 5:8).

Paul writes

"Christ Jesus came into the world to save sinners, And I am the foremost of sinners."

(1 TIMOTHY 1:15).

John writes

"If we say we have no sin, we deceive ourselves, and the truth is not in us. If we confess our sin, he is faithful and just, and will forgive us our sins ..."

(1 JOHN 1:8, 9).

Human and divine forgiveness

FORGIVEN? THEN FORGIVE

There is the closest possible connection between human and divine forgiveness. So much so, that he who is unforgiving has cut himself off from the forgiveness of God. Forgiven, we must be forgiving.

A CHALLENGING TRUTH

This presents us with a truth so challenging and even so threatening that we are not surprised to find that Chrysostom tells us that in his day there were many who suppressed this clause of the Lord's Prayer altogether.

NEW TESTAMENT TEACHING

- ❖ The connection between human and divine forgiveness is deeply ingrained into New Testament thought.
- ❖ The parable of the unforgiving debtor clearly lays down that an unforgiving man can hope for no forgiveness. *(Matthew 18:23-25)*
- ❖ As a man judges others, so he will be judged himself, and in matters of mercy he will get what he gives. *(Matthew 7:1, 2; Mark 4:24; Luke 6:37, 38)*
- ❖ It is the merciful who will receive mercy. *(Matthew 5:7)*
- ❖ "Judgement is without mercy to one who has shown no mercy." *(James 2:13)*.

RABBINIC TEACHING

This was in fact a legacy of Jewish thought. The rabbinic teaching is full of the conviction that the merciful man will receive the mercy of God, and that the merciless man has cut himself off from the mercy of God.

GAMALIEL

Gamaliel said: "So long as you are merciful, God will have mercy upon you, and if you are not merciful, he will not be merciful to you."

RABBI ZUTRA

Rabbi's Zutra's goodnight prayer before sleeping was: "Forgiven is everyone who has done me an injury."

THE DAY OF ATONEMENT

The Day of Atonement was the day on which the grand act of atonement for sins known and unknown, sins realized and sins unrealized, the total sin of the community was carried out in the Temple, and which continues to be observed by almost every Jew in this day.

Yet it is laid down that the Day of Atonement is unavailing unless a man has appeased and sought the pardon of the neighbor whom he has wronged. Maybe the noblest statement of this is in The Wisdom of Ben Sirach:

"Forgive your neighbor the wrong he has done, and then your sins will be pardoned when you pray."

RABA

"*Whom does God forgive? Him who overlooks the transgressions of others.*"

"*So long as a man remains in his stiffness God does not forgive him.*"

"*Whenever you have pity God forgives you.*"

"*Learn to receive suffering, and to forgive those who insult you.*"

Dare we pray this petition?

A CERTAIN DANGER

It becomes clear that there is in this petition a certain danger. "Forgive us our debts, as we forgive our debtors." The petition asks God to forgive us as we forgive others. This can only mean that if we are unforgiving, if we pray this when we are in a state of bitterness towards a fellowman, we are deliberately asking God *not* to forgive us.

"I WILL NOT FORGIVE"

Luther connects this petition with the saying in the Psalms which says of the wicked man: "Let his prayer be counted as sin!" *(Psalm 109:7)*. When this prayer is prayed by a bitter and unforgiving man it becomes a sin.

> "Psalm 109:7 says his prayer will be a sin in the sight of God; for what else canst thou mean when thou sayest, 'I will not forgive', and yet standest before God with thy Pater Noster, and babblest, 'Forgive us our debts, as we forgive our debtors', than, 'O God, I am thy debtor, and I also have a debtor; I am not willing to forgive him, therefore do thou also not forgive me: I will not obey thee though thou shouldst declare me pardoned; I would rather renounce thine heaven and everything else, and go to the devil'?" *Martin Luther*.

It is a dreadful thought that a man should ask God not to forgive him, and yet that is precisely what the unforgiving man does when he prays this prayer.

TAHITI

In the South Sea Islands in Tahiti it was Robert Louis Stevenson's custom to have family worship each day and in it to have the Lord's Prayer. One day in the middle of the prayer he rose from his knees and left the room. His wife hurried after him thinking that he was ill. "What is the matter?" she asked. "Are you ill?"

"No," he answered, "but I am not fit to pray the Lord's Prayer today!"

How often that must be true of all of us! Of all the prayers the Lord's Prayer can least be used unthinkingly.

GENERAL OGELTHROPE

Once General Oglethorpe remarked to John Wesley:

*"I never forgive",
to which Wesley
answered:
"Then I hope, sir,
you never sin."*

SELF-EXAMINATION

A man has to examine himself before he dares to pray this prayer, for in this petition a man becomes nothing less than his own judge.

As Chrysostom had it: "God makes you arbiter of the judgement; as you judge yourself, so he will judge you." There is a very real sense in which we are every day engaged in judging ourselves.

The condition for forgiveness

THE FORGIVING SPIRIT

There is no evading the principle that the condition of forgiveness is the forgiving spirit.

NO FELLOWSHIP BETWEEN OPPOSITES

Long ago Gregory of Nyssa *(Sermons on the Lord's Prayer 5)* pointed out that it could not be otherwise for the very simple and the very fundamental reason that there can be no fellowship between opposites.

- ❖ "It is impossible that a wicked man should be intimate with a good man.
- ❖ Or that someone wallowing in impure thoughts should be friends with someone who is perfectly pure.
- ❖ Thus a callous man trying to approach God is far from the divine charity.
- ❖ Therefore it is absolutely necessary that a man who approaches the charity of God should rid himself of callousness."

GOD'S NATURE

The very nature of God is such that between him and the unforgiving man there is a self-erected barrier.

A SELF-ERECTED BARRIER

- ❖ It is impossible that a merciless man should have fellowship with the divine mercy,
- ❖ or a loveless man should have fellowship with the divine love,
- ❖ or an unforgiving man with the God whose name is Savior and who delights to forgive.

KIN TO GOD

In this prayer there is laid upon us the duty of forgiving the sins of others. And this fact is for ever true, that a man is never closer and more kin to God than when he forgives a fellow man.

CONCLUSION

Forgive us our debts as we forgive our debtors — herein we confess our own sin, and herein we accept the fact that only the forgiving can be forgiven. As Paul had it: "Be kind to one another, tenderhearted, forgiving one another, as God in Christ forgave you" *(Ephesians 4:32)*.

A Jewish rabbi once said: "He who hears himself cursed, and has the opportunity to stop the man who curses him, and yet keeps silence, makes himself a partner with God."

We are disciples of him who prayed for forgiveness for those who were nailing him to a cross *(Luke 23:34)*. If we would imitate our Lord, and if we would be kin to God, we must forgive, and he who forgives will find for himself the forgiveness of God.

CHAPTER EIGHT

The Ordeal of Temptation

Two puzzling questions

It would be true to say that this is the most natural and instinctive petition in the Lord's Prayer. It is, says Chrysostom, the natural appeal of human weakness and human danger.

I How can we pray this petition?
How can we reasonably pray not to be led into temptation when in point of fact temptation is so integral to human existence on earth that we cannot conceive of life without it?

As Origen pointed out *(On Prayer 29.5)*, "Has anyone ever thought man to be beyond temptations of which he was aware from the day he attained to reason? Is there any time when a man is sure that he has not to struggle against sinning?" It is quite simply impossible to think of human existence without temptation.

THE VALUE OF TRIAL

Further, in Greek the word *trial* and the word *temptation* are the same word (*peirasmos*); and again and again the Bible points out the supreme value of trial.

- ❖ "When he has tried me," said Job, "I shall come forth as gold" *(Job 23:10)*.
- ❖ "Count it all joy, my brethren," said James, "when you meet various trials, for you know that the testing of your faith produces steadfastness" *(James 1:2)*.
- ❖ "In this," writes Peter, "you rejoice, though now for a little while you may have to suffer various trials, so that the genuineness of your faith, more precious than gold which though perishable is tested by fire, may redound to praise and glory and honor at the revelation of Jesus Christ" *(1 Peter 1: 6, 7)*.

In all these cases the word for trial is *peirasmos*, which is the very same word as is used for *temptation* in this clause of the Lord's Prayer.

II Does God lead us into temptation?

When we come to think of it, this is on the face of it an extraordinary prayer to pray, for in what sense can we ever believe that God would lead us into temptation? How could God ever be responsible for the attempt to seduce man into sin?

> ### LIFE WOULD BE SO DIFFERENT WITHOUT TEMPTATION
>
> *The undoubted teaching of life is that life is inconceivable without temptation, and the undoubted teaching of Scripture is that, if temptation were removed from life something irreplaceable would be lost with it.*

Meanings of the word temptation

THE VERB *PEIRAZEIN*

If we examine the verb *peirazein*, from which the noun *peirasmos*, (temptation) is derived, we will get the basic idea which lies behind this petition better. It may be said that the Greek verb *peirazein* has all the many senses of the English verb *to try*.

I To test loyalty

In the Bible *peirazein* is often used of God's testing of men to see whether or not their faith is genuine, loyal, and true. It is forbidden to listen to a false prophet or to a dreamer of dreams.

- ❖ When such a man emerges, "The Lord your God is *testing* you to know whether you love the Lord your God with all your heart and with all your soul" *(Deuteronomy 13:3)*.
- ❖ So God *tested* Abraham by seeming to demand the sacrifice of Isaac *(Genesis 22:1)*.
- ❖ God does not allow us to be *tested* beyond that which we can bear *(1 Corinthians 10:13)*.

II To trap

Peirazein is frequently used in the New Testament of the action of men who maliciously cross-examine or otherwise test someone with the deliberate intention of catching him out or making him incriminate himself. In this sense it is repeatedly used of the Scribes and Pharisees asking Jesus questions which were designed to entrap him *(Matthew 4:1-11)*.

III. To lead into sin

Peirazein is frequently used of the direct and deliberate seduction to sin which in English is the normal meaning of the word tempt. Husband and wives are not to deny each other their natural rights except by agreement, "lest Satan tempt you through lack of self-control."
(1 Corinthians 7:5).

In this sense Satan is pre-eminently *ho peirazon,* the tempter. It is thus that the Devil tempted Jesus in the wilderness *(Matthew 4:1-11).*

CHRISTIAN CONCEPT OF TEMPTATION

From all this certain truths emerge about the Christian concept of temptation.

- ❖ Temptation is universal and inescapable, part and parcel of the human condition.
- ❖ Temptation is not outside the plan and purpose of God.
- ❖ There is in temptation always an element of probation. Temptation is always essentially a test. Even when it is a seduction to sin, it is still a test of a man's resistance power.

It thus becomes true to say that temptation is not so much the penalty of manhood as it is the glory of manhood. It is that by which a man is made into the athlete of God.

Lead us not into temptation

AUGUSTINE

Augustine says that there were manuscripts of the New Testament in Latin in his day which rendered this clause: "Do not allow us to be led into temptation." It may well be that this is the correct interpretation. The Syrian version of the New Testament renders this clause: "Do not *make us enter into* temptations."

EXCELLENT SENSE

Here is an interpretation which gives us excellent sense, for in this case the meaning would be:

❖ Keep us from flirting with temptation.
❖ Keep us from situations in which temptation will get its chance.
❖ Defend us from the assaults of temptation which come from our own nature and from the seductions of others.
❖ Defend us from the attacks of the world, the flesh and the devil.

NO NEEDLESS EXPOSURE

It would be a prayer that neither by our own weakness nor by the malice of others we may be brought into life situations in which we are foolishly and sometimes needlessly exposed to the attack of temptation. It would be a prayer in which we ask God to be the defender and the guardian of our faith, our loyalty and our purity.

LOGIC OR HEART?

It may be that in all our efforts at explanation we are

allowing theological logic to take
precedence over the natural human
reaction of the heart.

DON'T PUSH ME TOO HARD

To take a very simple human analogy
and to put it in very colloquial terms,
we can easily imagine a student saying
to his teacher, or an athlete saying to
his trainer, never doubting the love of
the teacher or the good intent of the
trainer: "Go easy with me! Don't push
me too hard!"

AN INSTINCTIVE APPEAL

It may well be that this is
the best way in which to
approach this petition. It
may be best simply to see
it in the instinctive
appeal of the man who
knows how weak he is
and how dangerous life
can be, and who takes his
own peril to the
protection of God. For
the theologian the
theological problem may
be there; for the human
being the theological
problem is lost in the
instinctive appeal of the
human need.

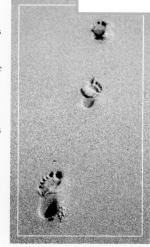

DOES GOD TEMPT ANYONE?

*As Tertullian
(On Prayer 8) said:*

*"Far be the thought
that the Lord should
seem to tempt anyone,
as if he were ignorant
of the faith of any, or
else were eager to
overthrow it."*

Deliver us from evil

VARIATION IN TRANSLATION

The translations in this clause are divided between: Deliver us from evil, in the general sense of the term, and, Deliver us from the Evil One in the sense of the Devil, the personal power of evil.

The Greek can equally well mean either, and in point of fact the variation in translation makes very little difference to the meaning.

THE EVIL ONE

It is well to understand what the biblical writers understand by the Evil One. The Evil One goes under two names in the Bible.

I Satan
Sometimes he is called *Satan*. The word *satan* was not originally a proper name; it originally meant an *adversary* in the ordinary human sense of the term. A *satan* is simply an adversary. Satan is characteristically the Adversary of man.

II Devil
Sometimes he is called the Devil. In Greek the word Devil is *diabolos*. *Diabolos* was originally neither a proper name nor a title. It is the normal Greek word for *slanderer*.

SATAN AND DEVIL

So then the word *Satan* describes the Adversary who is the prosecuting counsel against men. The word Devil, *diabolos*, describes the one who is *par excellence*, the slanderer.

And the two ideas are not so very different, because it is not so very far a cry from stating the case against a man to fabricating a case against a man. The aim of the Evil One is by any means to cause a breach between man and God, to break the relationship between man and God. The Evil One is the personification of all that is against God and all that is out to ruin man in this life and in the life to come.

CONCLUSION

Lead us not into temptation, but deliver us from evil. This concluding petition of the Lord's Prayer does three things.

- ❖ First, it frankly faces the danger of the human situation.
- ❖ Second, it freely confesses the inadequacy of human resources to deal with it.
- ❖ Third, it takes both the danger and the weakness to the protecting power of God.

GOD IS MY GUARDIAN

And when we do all this we can say with Cyprian *(The Lord's Prayer 27):*

"When we have once asked for God's protection against evil and have obtained it, then against everything which the devil and the world can do against us, we stand secure and safe. For what fear is there in this life to the man whose Guardian in this life is God?"

Epilogue

ITS OWN BUILT-IN EPILOGUE

The Lord's Prayer, as we commonly
might call its own built-in epilogu
ascription of praise: *"For thine is*
and the glory, for ever. Amen." (
The great value of this cor
that it reminds us of twc

❖ It reminds us to
❖ It reminds us
    have to giv

THINE IS THE

We end t
we are
alleg

W
the p
must liv
is living wr